MY LIFE THROUGH WORDS

BY

GINA DOUGLAS

DEDICATION

To those who came before me my ancestors

To those who stand beside me

To those who come after me learn from our

Mistakes

Table of Contents

SALUTE

A glass of wine,

A true delight to the palate.

Red, white, zinfandel and moscatto.

A relaxing sensation comes over me.

Bubble baths, candles and classical music,

A perfect way to end the day.

Salute

I TRIED

I try my best but it's not enough,

I give my heart and soul.

I know there are things I am not good at,

I try and it only leads me to hell.

I disappoint you and it hurts,

The look in your eyes devastates me.

I hold my tears and shame and disappointment in,

One day I will find my niche,

The those around me will be pleased.

PAIN

I hurt and you don't see it,
I cry and I hide it.
I scream inside my head,
So nobody can hear me.
My soul is in torment
One day I shall find peace.

INNER PEACE

I feel like a child full of innocence,

My soul is soaring free.

My eyes are wide open.

As I feel the breeze flowing through my hair.

I close my eyes and I can feel the sun kiss my face.

You walk over and call my name.

I turn to you and open my eyes.

You pull me to you and I can feel your passion

I taste it in your kisses

I feel it in your touch

I am a woman

You are a man

All our desires come to life

We are happy.

I AM WORTHY

You say that I am not the pretty one,

You make me feel ugly.

You say I am not the creative one,

Yet I do have hidden talents.

You say I am not the smart one,

Yet I have passed you.

You tell me I won't fit in and be laughed at,

I will never know.

I reconnect with my one love,

You tell me I will be a burden on him.

He says no and that he loves me.

You say he can't love me. I am not worthy.

I say I am worthy of him and his love.

YOU'RE THE ONE

I've loved you for so long,

Yet you never noticed me.

I forgave you for we were young,

You went to college and played football.

I went into the military and was trained.

You worked hard and played hard.

I worked hard to survive.

Yet after all these years,

You still make my heart race

You're the man I've always dreamed of

I am yours and you are mine forever.

DREAMING

I look towards the sky and watch as
The stars twinkle and dance throughout the
Night.
I look at you and see the twinkle in
Your eyes and that it makes my heart dance.
As the minutes turns into hours and
The hours turns into day and then into weeks.
The twinkle in your eyes turns into fear,
Your kisses have become less filled with passion
And filled more with friendship.
I long and scream out your name to hold me
And kiss me like you use to.
I know the fear you hold inside because I'm afraid
Too and I know that your love for me and your
Strong arms will keep me safe throughout the
Night.
In the end we fall asleep in each other's arms.

THE RING

The sapphires are bluer than the oceans.
The diamonds are more brilliant than the stars at
Night.
They come together just as I came to you.
It is symbolic of us and our love.
It is my dream engagement ring
When the time comes you have agreed to using
This ring
It is my dream wedding ring
When it does happen this ring will be with us
The ring is symbolic of our journey together
Through life.

FRIENDS

You can call each other and not get upset

For that call at 2:30 in the morning.

They will listen when you need to talk.

They will sit an cry with no questions asked.

They will pick you up should you fall.

Their love for you is unconditioned.

True friends are few and far in between.

GRIEF

Why do we grieve?
Is it really because you passed?
Is it more like you left me behind?
I know it's selfish on my part.
I don't want to go on without you.
I talked about your passing more than once
You would become whole and no pain
My heart was broken and withdrew from life.
We made a lot of memories
They all brough me comfort at times
You are still missed
You are still loved
You are still needed.

SHE AND I

She and I are not friends,
Yet we are not enemies.
We don't know each other,
But we know of each other.
She is old and weathered,
I am younger and living life.
We are the same,
We are different.
You are his past,
I am his present and future.
Your memory is fading,
Ours is fresh and new.
Say goodbye and live your life.
While we start ours together.

DEATH

I feel funny.

Whats happening to me?

I'm cold.

Its dark.

I feel myself floating.

I feel free.

I feel warm

The warmth is from the light

Its so bright and beautiful

I feel healed, no pain.

Its time for me to rest but I'm not tired.

I hear a voice but see no one.

Welcome home my child.

This is your eternal life.

MY SISTER

My sister is a very beautiful lady,

She is beautiful inside and out.

She is a woman and a child,

She is a mother and a friend.

She enjoys the simple things in life,

She is a rock for her children.

She is there for her grandchildren.

When she sees someone hurting,

She is the first to offer a helping hand.

She wants little in life.

She wants the security of her own home.

Her children to be happy and successful.

She wants the love that her boyfriend has to offer

She wants everyone around her to be happy and safe,

Things like a smile when she sees her baked good are eaten.

A glass of a good wine while enjoying a sunset.

Meeting friends for dinner.

The love of her boyfriend, family and friends.

She is happy and blessed.

I am glad she is my sister.

INVISIBLE

I sit here

You don't see me

I speak

You don't hear me

I cry

It doesn't have any effect

I leave

No one notices

I die

No one shows up

I go to heaven

God says

Welcome home child

I see you

ALONE

I sit beside you

Yet we don't speak

I lay beside you

Yet you don't hold me

Even though we are together

We are still alone in our heads

When I am away from you

It is like a dagger piercing my heart

The loneliness is unbearable

Death would be better than the pain I feel

A pain that runs tomy very core

The feelings of loneliness are intensified

I can't bear this

I run back to you

To find your arms wide open

Welcoming me back

A passionate kiss

A tight hug

We sit and talk

Work things out

We both realize

Neither one of us is alone anymore

We have each other.

I JUST DID

I had a crush on you in elementary school.

You look at me surprised. Why didn't you tell me?

I just did.

I was infatuated with you in junior high.

You look at me bewildered. Why didn't you tell me/

I just did.

I was in love with you in high school.

You just looked at me. Why didn't you tell me/

I just did.

I look at you from across the room.

You look at me and tell me you're in love with me.

I look at you and ask why didn't you tell me?

I just did.

TWO BECOME ONE

In a matter of months,

Two hearts began to beat as one.

I took you from your home,

After not seeing you for years.

Two lonely people found love and happiness.

We took your things from the house you lived in,

Put them in the house I lived in.

We made a home together.

Our hearts were married to each other.

For months we have been happy,

We have gone from existing to living.

No more lonliness.

We have accepted the good, the bad and the ugly.

In each other.

Our souls have become one.

A new challenge has been opened to us,

We have accepted the challenge together.

Our lives together is full and vibrant,

We were two and now we are one.

YOUR NOT MY MOTHER

You are not my mother,

You are simply the person

That gave birth to me.

At an early age

You gave me away

Your life was more important to you

Then caring for the life that you produced

You taught me at an age age

The art of pleasure

Ishould have been having sleep overs

And doing the things that normal girls do.

You gave me to an older woman

So, I could be broken in

I didn't want this

I wanted to be accepted and loved

My mother loved me and is she is not you

To you I was a money maker not a child

You allowed your boyfriends to do as they wish

I paid the price

I carried your cross and the burden that with it

My mother taught me how to be a strong woman

How to be respectable and think for myself

The love of my life taught me that I am beautiful

Inside and out

He taught me about love that is unconditional

All I can say is you are not my mother.

JONAH

When I first saw you

I couldn't believe my eyes

Here you were

In a kennel

Nothing but matted hair

You weighed next to nothing

I took you home that night

Couldn't believe how you stayed beside me

You got groomed

Three pounds of hair gone

You weighed 2.5 pounds

Two years later

You gained weight and started living life

You were eighteen

Fiesty and full of love

You are home

You are loved

You belong to us

Welcome home our fur baby.

I'M FREE

Sitting on a plane

Gazing out the window

Flying thru the clouds

Feeling at peace

Glimpses of the ground

Has my mind reeling

It's a farm I can tell

But to me it looks like a pattern

Could it be a quilt?

Could it possibly be something I could make?

An afghan maybe?

Designs and colors

All I need

My creative juices are flowing.

Then I see the trees on the hills

The leaves are turning

Reds and oranges and golds

I see blankets

My mind is free

I am free.

SPIRITS AMONG US

The alive are dead

The dead are the alive

We are together yet we are separate

We are good

We are evil

We are black

We are white

The alive are dead

The dead are alive.

WHY DAD

You were supposed to love me,

I am your only daughter.

You made lewd comments on my body

You would say if only you weren't my daughter

If you only I didn't have to look in the mirror

Why dad couldn't you love me

Why dad couldn't you accept me

Why dad couldn't you give me the love

That I needed

Be the father that a young girl would need

You set the stage for the rest of my life

You showed me how a man was to treat a woman

So I went for men who were like you

Why dad couldn't you love me?

PATIENCE

I have never been known to have much

When I started to grow up later in life

I started to understand

When I became a woman.

Men taught me to be patient.

As a mother I really needed to learn a lot.

This test I failed.

As an older woman dealing with dementia

And cancer with both my aunt and grandmother

Patience was needed around the clock

I did pass this test

With the man I love

Patience comes naturally.

NOT MY MAN

You can stroke his ego

You can never win.

Show him your goods

He will simply turn his head.

And walk away

Bat your eyes

Or cook his meal

He will simply ignore you.

Promise him the world

He will tell you he has the world

Offer him love

He will let you know he has more than any man

Can ask for

You can try

You will never get my man.

WHAT USE TO BE

Your eyes meet from across the room

And those old feelings for him are there

Stronger than ever

He walks over and put his arms around you

You shiver from the electricity running thru

Your body

He asks how you've been

You tell him your great

You look into his eyes

Something is different

You can't put your finger on it

Then it comes to you

He's in love but it's not with you

It's now that you realize what use to be

Is simply that

What use to be.

WHO AM I?

I am someone's daughter and granddaughter

I am also someone's mother and grandmother.

I am your aunt and sister

I am a lover, a friend, a wife and a caregiver.

I am a groomer and a vet to our furbabies.

Someone is in need I step up to assist.

I am your legacy.

Most of all

I am a woman in love.

INVISIBLE WOUNDS

You can't see them on the surface

But they run deep inside.

You do not talk about it

You feel no one would understand.

But if you told, you would only be judged.

You get told it never happened,

All you want is validation.

The damage and scars are buried deep within,

You can't seem but they are there.

My wounds are invisible but they are there.

ANGELS AMONG US

Many angels walk the earth and you walk beside
Them daily,
They are short and tall, thin and fat.
They have brown hair, blonde hair and no hair at
All.
They come into our lives when we need them the
Most.
They come as a friend, lover and maybe a relative.
I have had many angels in my life who have taught
Me lessons.
My grandmother, a rescued dog even a friend or
Two.
They would point me in the direction that I needed
To go.
Yet it is always up to me to listen to their
Guidance.
They taught me about compassion and patience.
They even taught me about love.
I do believe there are angels among us.

MOMMA K

You loved him as a child,

I love him as a man.

You tended to him when he was young,

I tend to his needs in his senior years.

You taught him to dance,

I enjoy his arm around me when we have a chance.

You told him girls would always want him,

As a girl I did, as a woman I want him on many

Levels.

Your job raising him is over.

I promise you momma k,

I will always be there for him and loving him.

The way his siblings and you have accepted me,

My family has accepted him unconditionally.

Thank you for raising him to be the man that he is,

The one love of my life.

Thank you, momma k.

THEN CAME YOU

I thought I forgot how to laugh,

You taught me how to laugh again.

When I shed a tear or feel fear,

You wipe it away or chased it away.

Then came you.

At night when I am lying in bed,

I think of you until sleep over takes me.

As dreams come and go,

You are always there to protect me.

Then came you.

As we travel thru our golden years,

Side by side and hand in hand.

I see your smile and I feel happiness like no other,

But now as I turn to see you smile,

I finally realize you are gone.

And I walk these roads alone once again,

Then came you.

ALONE AGAIN

I had always been alone in my life,
I thought that was just how life was.
Then I noticed how much others were laughing.
I never dated much didn't see any sense in it.
So, I never learned how to be with anyone,
I married and felt so alone in the marriage.
His beatings started and so did his cheating.
I left.

My next four relationships were abusive and
Lonely,
Then you came back into my laugh,
You brought with you love and laughter.
I then realized I wasn't lonely anymore.
Then it happened and I couldn't believe it
You were gone.
I stayed with you until your last breath.

I GAVE UP

I am a cutter, I like to cut,

I like the relief it brings.

The feelings of euphoria are addictive.

The gratification is instant.

The high doesn't last long.

This is not a sucide attempt,

This is just a release.

I did it for the thrill and the high,

Then the day came that others feared,

I cut myself unintentionally to deep.

I felt the euphoria come and go rapidly,

I felt the warmth of the blood run down my

Fingers,

I felt what seemed like my soul leaving me,

I crumpled to the hard cold tile floor.

This had never happened before.

I'm dying I cut too deeply,

I feel the warmth of the light take me,

I just laid there and died. I just gave up.

MY PASSING

I sit here thinking about my end,

I know when the time comes, I'll be alone.

That's ok I've basically been alone all my life.

I've been alone with just my dogs,

That's been ok so far with me.

I know when that time comes there won'b be

Anyone,

No one will travel to my home,

No one will shed a tear when I am gone.

No one to stand at my grave site.

No one to receive my military flag.

My dogs are in my casket and so is my husband,

I hope they will all be together.

I can see them all and so many more.

It is my turn to pass.

WHO AM I NOW?

I use to be a soldier, now I'm a disabled vet,

I use to be a trucker then a trucker's wife.

I use to be a wife now I'm a divorcee,

I use to be a caregiver then they all died.

I am alone again then you came into my life,

Where I would shed tears you can find laughter,

Where I would find lonliness you can find joy.

Now when I smile it is real and I am happy.

OUR FIRST TIME TOGETHER

(Our Wedding Night)

As I feel his hot breath on my neck,

I can also feel his lips on mine.

He takes my breath away.

He slowly and sensuously caresses my side,

I feel the hunger for his kiss deep inside of me.

He pushes against me, and his hand is on my hip,

I can feel both his hardness and his thickness.

I turn towards him, and he lifts himself above me,

I spread my legs and pull him towards me.

I could feel his weight on top of me,

I could feel as he guided his hard manhood inside

Of me.

My body quivers and trembles,

His thrusts are hard and quick.

We are both going primal,

As he expl0des inside me, I thrust my hips and bite

His shoulder.

My body trembles as I lose control,

Our first time together was more than I ever

Expected,

We are both happy and satisfied.

MY BIRTH MOTHER

You're a bitch, it's always about you,
You're a whore it's always about who your
Sleeping with.
Your're selfish its about what you can get,
You have always made it clear you're the victim,
Yet that's not true.
We all agree your no victim.
You left one of us in a hospital.
You left one of us in another country.
The other two were taken by the judge and given
To your mother.
You think everyone turned us against you but you
Turned us against you.
Yet you give none of us credit for making up our
Own minds.
We are not stupid.
You are not our mom.
You are just the incubator.

MY BUCKET LIST

My bucket list is like no other,

I want to go to ireland and admire the men.

Then on to scotland to admire the god like bodies

Let's face it pro wrestlers like finn and drew are

Perfect examples of this.

I want to explore my ancestors,

To wear the colors that were established for

Them.

I want to go skydiving and feel free.

I want to go to england and see the family castle.

I want to live my life without judgement.

These are the things I want to do.

This is my second bucket list.

MY MORNING CUP OF COFFEE

I can smell your aroma as you brew,

It tells me everything is going to be ok.

When you've stopped brewing,

I just stand there and take in your aroma.

My mouth is watering for that first sip,

To feel its heat as it hits my tongue.

That first taste puts a smile on my face,

Looking out the windows seeing the mountains

And the sun.

No better way to start the day,

Then with my morning cup of coffee.

GOODBYE MY LOVE

Doug,

It felt and seemed like a dream when you and I
Reconnected, since high school. I wanted for my
First kiss to come from you. Unfortunately, I
Had to wait 41 years for that to happen. March of
2019, I got my first kiss from you. I had never in my
Life had I been kissed that way. That march you
Put a blue sapphire ring on my finger and you
Asked me to be yours and I said yes. I moved you to
Tennessee that year. You were in awe of the
Mountains and felt like you were coming home.
You loved the life we had together. Then one day
You became sick. You argued with me about going
To the hospital but you gave in and went. An hour
Later you were gone. I don't understand. We were
To be married in 3 weeks. My whole life changed.
It's been almost 2 years and I must move on. My
Heart is still broken. Time has come to say good
Bye and to let you know I still love and miss you.
I wish you were here.
Love   G

SOUL MATE

When I close my eyes,

I can see you.

I can see me.

I can see the love we have for each other,

I can feel the passion between us.

I can feel the touch of your hand as it caresses

My face,

You stand and offer your hand and lead me to

Dance.

I can taste your kisses,

Sweet yet slightly guarded.

I'm in love with him,

He's in love with me,

We are soulmates.

BROKEN CHILD

I am a child,
I was born innocent,
You took that away from me.
I had no choice,
My childhood was taken,
It was full of abuse and pain,
I am broken.
I am a broken child.

BROKEN WOMAN

You say that you love me,

Yet you break my bones,

You blacken my eyes,

You want to be intimate,

I lay there with fear and hate in my heart.

I am bound by your chains,

I try to break them and fail,

You die and I am free,

I am broken.

I am a broken woman.

GOODBYE TOOTS

When I lost you, my world collapsed,
You left me behind.
I wanted to go with you,
You came to me and I am comforted.
You tell me I am doing fine.
I know I made you proud,
My heart is shattered.
I am full of sorrow,
You depended on me,
I feel as though I failed.
You loved me as if I were your own,
I loved you as my mother.
You are missed.
You are still loved.
Good bye till we see each other again.

IN LOVE

I am in love,

I am soaring thru the blue skies.

I am dancing on the clouds.

The sun is warm on my face.

My life is brighter.

My soul that was once in turmoil has found

Peace,

My confidence has grown.

I am strong and in love.

ANGELS

I see them brightly glowing,

I close my eyes and I feel their love

Surrounding me,

I feel their warmeth as if they are wrapping

Their arms around me,

They speak of their love for me,

They share their wisdom with me and guide me

Through lifes journey,

They bless me,

They are my angels.

ME

As I look out the window

And listen as the rain hits the glass.

My mind wanders thru time

As memories come flooding back.

Some good and some bad,

Yet all of these expierences have made me

Who I am,

I am strong.

I am independent.

I am real.

I am me.

PEACE OF MIND

Where do I find peace?

Before you, I found it in the mountains,

Before you I found it in nature.

I found it in my faith.

I found peace in my dogs.

I found peace in discovering myself.

They you came along and I found love.

I found peace within you and your love.

Most of all I found peace within myself.

THE FLAME

Sometimes it appears to be dancing,

Sometime it appears to be perfectly still,

Sometimes its short and times tall.

At times you can see colors such as red yellow

Orange, green and blue.

It is soothing and beautiful,

It is the flickering of the flame.

WHO IS MY HUSBAND

H is for my hero

U is for his unconditional love

S is for his sensitivity

B is for his shoulders they are so so broad

A is for the admiration that I see in his eyes

N is for his living in the now moment

D is for his total devotion for us

These are only a few reasons as to why I love him

There are so many more

I LOVE YOU

GOOD BYE MY LOVE

I have loved you with a broken heart,
When you leave me, I will be the one with
The broken heart.
You are freee of the pain you felt,
I am the one who is devistated.
You always dept your promises to me,
I promise to join you soon.
The greatest gift a man can give a woman he
Loves is his name,
I loved you unconditionally and your arms and
Love comforted me.
Now that your gone I am comforted by memories
And a name,
Your name the most priceless that you had that
Was yours.
You honored me by asking me to have it,
I told you yes and you made it happen.
I have lost your body,
I have your name.
I miss you and I will soon be with you.

LOVE IS?

Love is kind and generous,

Yet there can be a rough patch.

Love is worth fighting for.

Love is nurtured so that it can grow.

So, it will bloom between two people.

Love is destined for all,

It is a light that brightens up the darkness.

Love is as gentle as a cool breeze on a summer day

Love is like a cold drink of water,

It can refresh the soul.

Love is wonderful.

HEART BROKEN

I've heard you say twice that you and your

Dog will be fine.

Whatever happened to you saying we will be fine.

You say everything is messed up.

You act as if I had done something to cause this.

You seperated our things,

It feels like you're pushing me out and away.

I love you and don't want this to end.

Your words and actions say you do.

I am heartbroken.

SUCCESS

You are the one who made sure I was safe at night,

You made sure I had clean sheets on my bed and

Food in my belly.

You taught me to use my brains and not my body

To succeed in life,

I was taught to think for myself and to seek out

Solutions in life.

I am you but younger.

I am alive and I am happy.

I am living my dreams.

I am a success because of you.

A LETTER TO MY DAUGHTER

MY DAUGHTER,

When I found out I was pregnant with you I had

So many emotions running thru me. I had had a

Pregnancy test done the month before and it

Was negative. I was in a car accident the

Following month and found out in an xray that I

Was already in my second trimester with you. Boy

Did you scare the dr. A few months later you came

Into the world and about fourteen hours later

We went home. Your great grandma and your

Great great grandma were both present. We were

All happy that we finally had a girl. You were

Always so tiny.

I went away but always thought of you and your

Brother and I loved you so much. Almost three

Decades later you contacted me. You had a lot of

Questions and I answered as honest as I could. I

Always wanted for you to be happy. I always

Wanted for you to find a successful man and fall

In love and have your own family. Sometimes life

Doesn't deal us a good hand and we have to play

The hand we were dealt. You were dealt the same

Hand I was in life. For that I am sorry. Now your

A beautiful young woman who has had her own

55

Success in life and I'm sure you will have many
More. I will always be there for you and you know
My door is always open for you. I am so very proud
Of you.
LOVE,
MOM

BIGFOOT

Tall and hairy,

Fantasy or fiction.

Interdeminsional or of this world,

Male, female and juvenile.

Smarter than man and even more dangerous,

Man, hunts them out of fear.

He avoids man out of survival,

He's not in just one country,

He's all over the world.

He is known by many names,

I'm a believer.

I believe in bigfoot.

IS THERE HOPE FOR US?

Looking up at the stars and wondering about
Other forms of life,
I find it hard to believe we are the only ones here.
Please don't tell me we are considered the
Intelligent life forms here,
Boy are we in big trouble.
I know that life exists among the stars.
I know that some live among us.
I once knew a man who was from the stars
He was sent here as punishment for a crime he had
Committed.
He was most definitely sent to hell.
I'm sure he wasn't the first or the last.
They conform to look like us,
They act like us,
They even learn to eat like us.
So see we are not the only ones out there.
There could be hope for us yet.

DEAR GOD

DEAR GOD,

My understanding is that your allegedly a
Loving and merciful god. If that is true, then why
Do you forsake those who are lost and confused?
Why do you allow deacons, elders and priests to
Molest children in your churches and in your
Name? When these young people lose their faith
Because of what happened to them, do you
Condemn the young person or do you hold the
Predator accountable for you losing a soul?
Whenever I lost someone that I loved and cried
Out to you where were you? I lost my faith due to
Your followers, will you hold them accountable?
I don't understand how you can allow children to
Be harmed in and out of your churches. This
Doesn't sound like a loving and merciful god to
Me. This doesn't sound like the god I was taught
About. So where is this god? I don't see him
Anymore

WORLD HAS GONE CRAZY

The world has gone crazy,

What happened to the world I grew up in?
You can no longer play outside until dark,
You hear about children missing daily.
Men, women and children being abducted,
Forced into prostitution, transporting drugs,
And even human trafficking.
We could go to school and be safe,
Now when you send them to school they may not
Come home.
Men don't want to work,
China releases a contagent that took many
Lives.
What has happened to the world and mankind.
The world has gone crazy.

A STITCH IN TIME

Short tight stitches,

Long basting stitches.

Squares from clothing no longer wearables.

Jennys dress, grandpas shirt, daddys trousers

And moms apron.

One stitch at a time.

Soon a new quilt for the bed before winter sets

In.

Jenny wore this dress when she fell off the swing

And broke her arm.

Grandpa wore this when jason was baptized.

Come to think of it that was the day you last

Wore these trousers.

Oh the memories are now just …

A stitch in time.

MY BROTHER

Tall and handsome,

Looks like a viking.

Physical and built,

A do it yourselfer.

A master on the grill.

Daddy to furbabies

And to the child.

Smart as a whip

And strength to boot.

Hes a dad, brother, uncle, friend and hero.

He's an army veteran,

I'm proud to say he's my brother.

A PIECE OF TRASH

You may think you're a man but your not.
You would take care of your responsibilities
If you were.
You would make sure that your loved ones had
A roof over their heads.
Not living in a tent, garage, shack or couch
Surfing.
You claim to have multiple jobs but barely work.
Always in bed and always getting high
You expect everyone to give it to you.
You expect everyone to get you cigarettes,
You act like your entitled.
Your entitled to a bullett or a beating.
You are not welcomed to my phone.
You are not welcomed to other family members
Homes also.
My dogs are accepted better than you.
You are nothing but a piece of trash.

FOXY AND FANCY

Foxy my handsome red fox,

Such a beautiful boy.

Well behaved and so loving,

He could only make his momma proud.

Protective yet gentle,

He and his sister are a husky mix.

Their first mom either passed or was placed some

Where.

These two gentle souls were surrendered to the

Humane society,

Unfortunately, they had to share the same kennel.

Fancy is foxys sister and she is black and tan.

She has the protective nature of a warrior.

She is the nurturing mother.

She and foxy are loved and safe and found their

Forever home together.

ZOE

Zoe was a silverback terrier

She looked like a larger yorkie

She was adopted by my aunt

Then my grandmother and I inherited her

Grandma passed and it was her and I

She loved ice cream and m&m's

She survived about eightteen month after

Grandma

Like the others that have passed she too will

Be placed in my coffin

I'm glad she allowed me to be her last mom

Till we are reunited at rainbow bridge

Love and miss you baby girl

SPARKLE AND DAYO

You two have been with me the last twelve
Years.
It's been a true adventure so far
I am sure there are many more to come
Dayo, you have the face of a puppy
Short little legs and a lot of energy
Hard to believe you turn thirteen new years eve
Sparkles, you are my chunky love bug
You get so excited over everything
You make me laugh
When I cry you lick away my tears
You act silly and make me smile
I would be lost without the two of you
I love my poodles.

BEAR

When I first met you
I thought you were gonna eat me alive.
In turn I fell in love with you
I realized you were a big ole teddy bear
You were gentle, loving and very protective
The day I had to move you to rainbow bridge
Broke my heart
I know your dad was standing there waiting for
You
He loved you so much and worried about what
Would happen to you
I told him you would stay with me
He was happy about that and you did
You knew you were safe and loved
Now you are happy and healed
We miss you dearly
You are still loved handsome boy
I was proud to be your momma

MARY YOU WANNA

Got ya covers can be deceiving

This includes people, plants and animals

List could go on and on

Nothing wrong with being 420 friendly

My pain has lessoned

Me meds are fewer

My drs are supportive

My health is even better

I keep my stress and anxiety are lower

I am able to tap into my creative juices

It assists with writers block

It can take you on a mental vacation

Life is good and productive

THUNDERSTORMS

Dark clouds creeping over the mountains

Rumbling of thunder in the distance

Leaves on the trees turned downward to the

Ground

Birds are not flying

The sun is gone and stars are dark

A house shaking crack of thunder

Lightening dances all around

Rain coming down causing the creeks to flood

Perfect sleeping weather

After it has passed the earth smells clean

The world comes back to life

I love thunderstorms they are magical

LIFE IS GOOD

When you were here with me
I thought wow life is good
We never really did anything
But I was content and happy
We would sit and talk
And you would say
Life is good isn't it babe
I would respond with
Hell, yeah it is
Then you left and it isn't so good
For two years I could say
Life is good

I'M LOST

I am lost

I don't know where to go

I don't know what to do

I live in darkness

But where is the light

I am so cold

Where is the warmth

Why don't I know which way to go

I wish someone would find me

I'm scared and alone

Please help me

I'm lost

Gina Douglas

WHERE DO I GO FROM HERE

Where do I go from here
I have no idea
I have no direction in my life
I have no clue
Do I turn left or right
Do I laydown or stand up
Do live or do I die
Do look towards the sky
Or stay staring at the ground
Do I cry or laugh
Am I happy or sad
My only question is
Where do I go from here

LETTER TO MY OLDEST SON

You've angry since you were a child at everyone
Except for those who were responsible for your
Anger. I keep trying and I've apologized
Repeatedly. Things happened behind the scenes.
I heard about by mistake. Things that happened
To both you and I, unfortunately the one
Who was behind everything denies it to this
Day. You want me to do for you and when I
Do you become very abusive. As of today the
Abuse stops and so does my helping you. As of
Today it is goodbye. I love you but it's done.

MOM

LETTER TO MY YOUNGEST SON

I know you've been angry at me your whole
Lifeand that's understandable. I accept
The responsibility on my part of the
Situation. I accept the fact you hate me
And have respected your decision not to
Have a relationship with me. I was always there
When you asked for something. My door
Will always be open to you regardless
But like I told you I will never buy your love.

I DO LOVE YOU

MOM

LETTER TO MY GRANDSON

You are so young and full of innocence. You

Like to get into everything. Just like a boy.

There is so much in life for you to explore

And experience. My wish for you is that

You grow up happy and healthy. That you

Achieve all of your dreams. That you find real

True love and it lasts forever. I pray that

You will do at least one thing a day to make

Someone elses life a little brighter. All

Of these I pray for you and so much more.

I LOVE YOU

GRAMMA

LETTER TO MY GRANDDAUGHTER

You are the oldest of all of the grandchildren.
You have that timeless hollywood beauty
About you. You have goals and passion about
Life and you know where you want to be. I
Know without a doubt you will achieve all you
Want. You are a daughter, sister, granddaughter
And friend. I am so glad you reached out to
Me and I had the priviledge of getting to know
A pretty special young woman. I am so very proud
Of you.
LOVE

GRAMMA

LETTER TO MY DAD

I really didn't get to see you much a I was
Growing up. I was proud that you were a
Pro wrestler. They that when I pull my hair
Back I look like you. Your oldest son looks just
Like you and you look just like your dad. Yes I
Found him but it was to late. You even had a
Half brother and he has passed also. Things
Happened between us that never should have.
You made me feel I was a bad daughter and
Wouldn't be loved if I didn't give in. You
Apologized and asked me to forgive you and
I did. The damage was already done.

LETTER TO MY FRIENDS

You say that I'm your friend. You say that we
Are friends. Really? Seriously? Then please
My "friend" when you found out I had lost my
Husband why didn't you call? Why didn't you
Even send a text? Yet when you were going thru
Tough times I would call and check on you daily.
That's how I was taught. It always seems like I
Cared more about you that you did about me.
True friends are hard to find and fake friends
Are everywhere. My best friends are my brother
And sister. They are always there for me
Unconditionally. I treasure them both.

KNIGHTS OF THE HIGHWAY

Living like a gypsy, a nomad

A true wanderer.

Living a lifestyle like no other,

Following that black ribbon from coast to

Coast and border to border.

Truckers deliver everything that you

Can see, taste, hear, smell and touch.

They deliver babies on the side of the road.

First on the scene of accidents and save lives.

They miss birthdays and holidays.

They miss out on many firsts.

Next time you see a driver say thank you

Without them you would have nothing.

GARDENING

The feel of dirt under your nails
The smell of eart in your nostrils
Feeling the warmth of the sun as you
Place the seeds in the ground
Feeling the excitement of what could be
As your watering the seeds
I can picture the tomatio plants tall and
Strong
Green beans climbing the trellis
Cucumber and squash are plentiful
Watermelons are on their vines
I get excited with thoughts of canning
We will have peaches on the trees
We will never be hungry
The earth will always provide if
We will only take care of her
I love gardening

QUILTING

Long stitch, short stitch
Loose stitch, tight stitch
Machine stitch, hand stitch
Paperpiecing, appliques, solid colors
Prints and patterns
Backings and battings
They all tell a story
Some may say spring is here
Some may say merry christmas
If you go back in time
They would tell slaves whey they could
Hide or find food
They would know to go left or right
They knew who would help them
Quilting is a big part of our history
A big part of tradition
Will be a big part of our future also

HANDMADE

Sitting and thinking

Looking at books

Feeling the yarn

Smelling the fabric

What should I make

What should I do

This material would make a pretty top

This thread as a tablecloth

I see a quilt here

Oh and an afghan there

I love to make homemade gifts

Blood and tears go into each step

Everything is made with love

Everything is made for you

DREW MCINTYRE

(PRO WRESTLER)

Six foot five two hundred sixty pounds

The chiseled body of a greek god

Piercing eyes and kissablle lips

Sweat glistening on his chest, hard nipples,

With abs of steel

Perfect ass with thighs to bite

How I would love to fun my tongue over every

Inch of you.

Would love to make this man go primal.

Would love to make his fantasies come true

Let him do anything and everything

Make us both scream in ecstacy

Sexiest man alive to me

FINN BALOR

(PRO WRESTLER)

Handsome and irish

Babyface to heel

Five feet eleven and two hundred pounds

Firm body and tight ass

How I could kiss his lips and get lost

In his eyes

He could be my dominant master and

I his submissive slave

I would give the demon king

My soul with no regrets

I will follow you unto judgement day

GENEALOGY

Laying in bed at night

Wondering who I am

What makes me me?

This is my journey that I must

Embark on

I know who my grandparents are

I know who my great grandparents are

Who came before them?

One ancestor rode with jesse james

One ancestor was arrested for being a

Male witch during the salem witch trials

Another scouted for daniel boone and

Assisted with the wilderness trail

Some were cops, farmers and warriors

Things have become clearer for me

Now I teach genealogy

MY ROSE BUSH

My rose bush looks dead

It produces varigated purple roses

My husband died two years ago

His last gift to me was this bush

He said this out live him

I'm sorry I lost im but happy with the bush

Whenever I am down I can look at it

Seems like a new bud is producing

A new rose will be in full bloom

He said I would always have a rose from him

I do

I love my rose bush

It brings me comfort

It lets me know I am not alone

WHAT DOES TOMORROW HOLD

What does tomorrow hold?

Will there be a cure or even treatment

For diseases that there is nothing for today?

I know it won't be in my lifetime

Will it be in my grandchildrens lifetime?

My wish for tomorrow is that they won't have

To suffer as I have

Will there be tolerence or no tolerence

When we shall live with those

Who come from the stars

As I sit here and ponder

As my mind starts to wander

What does tomorrow hold?

SALEM WITCH TRIALS

Religious leaders fighting over congregations

Judges being bought off

Young girls pointing deceptive fingers

They accused men and women, young and old

Alike

Salem built on lies, deception, and the blood of

Innocents

Everything done by hypocrites in the name of god

All these years later nothig has changed

One of my ancestors was arrested for being

A male witch

As a member of the human race their actions

Embarassed by their actions of intolerance

As a sister witch I mourn the loss of my

Brothers and sisters

May your gentle souls finally find peace

NAMASTE

LET ME BE FREE

Let me be free

It's all I ask of thee

Be free of pain

Is all I ask to gain

To be free as the current of the river

To travel as the wind

In any direction as my spirit sees fit

To be free to feel the warmth of sun

Imagine my spirit walking in summerland

To soar on the wings of an eagle

To go higher than ive ever known

True peace and happiness

Just let me be free

Gina Douglas

POST TRAUMTIC STRESS
DISORDER

Post traumatic stress disorder

Goes by different names

Battle fatigue, shell shock, combat neurosis,

Combat disorder, combat fatigue

Ptsd make it without as much stigma

In my case it is from my military service

No I wasn't in combat but a prisoner of my own

Mind

My ptsd is secondary to the trauma affliated

With mst that I had suffered while in

Trauma is where ptsd is borne out of

An event that is life altering and the mind

Simply cant handle

There is no cure but ther is treatment

There is hope

WITCHES

My brothers and sisters

We all started this our spiritual walk it is a

Lifetime journey

We are healers, drs, and even advisors

We are harm no one

Yet we are the most misunderstood

We are feared and attacked due to ignorance

You want to kill us

We want to offer you a helping hand

A shoulder to cry on and an ear to hear your

Words

We come from all over the world

Like you we have good and bad

Unlike you we accept our beliefs and lives

Are different

Unlike you we don't judge you

We live in peace

LADY BALTIMORE

Beautiful and regal

True symbol of patriotism

She is an icon of survival

She is also a reminder of the

Evil men can do

Lady baltimore is a bald eagle

A true living miracle

She was shot in the eye and blinded

Shot in the wing and now can't fly

Shot in the beak and damaged

She was also in shot in her talons

She survived and lives in captivity

Fearing she couldn't fend for herself

So beautiful and graceful

Lady Baltimore

SACRIFICES

Nothing is to much for you

I gave up my heart

Knowing you would break it

I see your smile as it lights up a room

I can feel the tears as they roll down my

Cheek

I will go without eating so that your belly

Is full

You will have a warm comfortable bed

While I am cold at night

When you love someone

You can never sacrifice enough

Gina Douglas

SURVIVING DOMESTIC VIOLENCE

You degraded me and belittled me

You made me feel less than

You beat me and blackened my eyes

Broken bones and bruises

Thoughts of suicide runs through my mind

I have to get away

He's going to kill me

Because of you I married two more like you

Now I know I am more than

I am in control

I am empowered

I am strong

Now my advice to you is

Treat me like a lady or

I will kick your ass like a man

I am no longer a victim

I am a survivor

MICHIGAN

Sand dunes and beaches

Upper and lower peninsulas

A bridge connects the two

A bridge connects us to canada

We have evergreens and water

Any place you stand within a

Mile and a half of water

We have cities and casinos

Farms, orchards and ranches

We have all five great lakes

There is ice skating, skiing and snow

Mobiling in the winter time

Boating, skiing, horseback riding

Just to name a few for summer time

No matter what you like

No matter what your into

There is always plenty to do

TENNESSEE

Rolling hills and high mountain tops

The sun peaks over to say

A beautiful day awaits you

Breeze off the mountains

Makes the summer bearable

The energy is positive and rejuvenates

The bears and wolves and the eagles

All roam free

We even have bigfoot

If you dare to believe

This my home

My Tennessee

LOSS

Loss is the most devastating
And traumatic experience that
We will have to contend
With in our lifetimes
It hits us on many levels
Emotionally, mentally and physically
We give up and become depressed
We grieve and we get angry
We even feel emotions intensified
We have to feel in order to deal
We have to deal in order to heal

SELF DEFENSE

Loss is the most devastating

And traumatic experience that

We will have to contend

With in our lifetimes

It hits us on many levels

Emotionally, mentally and physically

We give up and become depressed

We grieve and we get angry

We even feel emotions intensified

We have to feel in order to deal

We have to deal in order to heal

MAKING DREAMS COME TRUE

Let's get realistic about this

Dreams don't come true just

Because you wish upon a star

They don't come true because

You have a rabbits foot in your pocket

Dreams come true because you dare to dream

Dreams come true because you

Put forth the effort to make them

Come true

Hard work and believing

In yourself is what makes

Dreams come true

Mine did

WICCA

What is wicca?

Wicca is a nature based

Alternative religion

It is a modern day religion

That is truly misunderstood

Those who follow this are judged

Harshly and by lies and untruths

Wiccans believe in do no harm

In all religions, cultures and lifestyles

There are good and bad

In wicca I have found peace

And happiness

I have found happiness without

Judgement

CRUISIN

Sitting on th deck

Sun shining down on my face

The mist blowing up on me

The breeze blowing thru my hair

A drink in my hand

I wonder about the vastness

Of the ocean and the secrets it holds

Whales jumping out of the water

Dolphins following the ship

I am happy, relaxed and at peace

I love cruising

QUEEN ELIZABETH II

Her royal highness queen elizabeth ii

She was a grand lady

She was a strong, independent woman

A globsl role model for women like me

She was tough yet gentle

She ruled for many decades

To the best of her abilities

She had only one love and when he passed

He broke her heart

She stood tall with her head held high

It is only my opinion that she died

From a broken heart

Her grandson did this beautiful lady no favors

They repeatedly compiled her heart break

I pray she is at peace and beside

Her one true love

In his own way

God did save the queen

www.ingramcontent.com/pod-product-compliance
Lightning Source LLC
La Vergne TN
LVHW052034080426
835513LV00018B/2315